1-07

DATE DUE

1-07

Vintage Cars
1919-1930

L. Michelle Nielsen

x1000r/min

CRABTREE PUBLISHING COMPANY
www.crabtreebooks.com

Crabtree Publishing Company
www.crabtreebooks.com

To my parents, Ben and Wendy, a driving force.

Coordinating editor: Ellen Rodger
Series editor: Rachel Eagen
Project Editor: Carrie Gleason
Editor: Adrianna Morganelli
Design and production coordinator: Rosie Gowsell
Cover design and production assistant: Samara Parent
Art direction: Rob MacGregor
Photo research: Allison Napier

Consultant: Kit Foster, automotive historian

Photo Credits: Bibliotheque des Arts Decoratifs, Paris, France, Archives Charmet/The Bridgeman Art Library: p. 13 (top); Private Collection, Archives Charmet/The Bridgeman Art Library: p. 19 (bottom left); Private Collection, Roger Perrin/The Bridgeman Art Library: p. 13 (bottom); Bettmann/Corbis: p. 7 (top), p. 9 (top right), p. 11 (bottom), p. 14, p. 15, p. 16, p. 17, p. 24, p. 25 (top); Condé Nast Archive/Corbis: p. 5 (top); Hulton-Deutsch Collection/Corbis: p. 31 (top); George D.

Lepp/Corbis: p. 29 (top); Craig Lovell/Corbis: p. 28; Minnesota Historical Society/Corbis: p. 5 (bottom); Joseph Sohm; ChromoSohm Inc./Corbis: p. 27; Swim Ink 2, LLC/Corbis: p. 18 (bottom right); The Granger Collection, New York: p. 19 (top right); National Motor Museum/HIP/The Image Works: p.10; National Motor Museum/Topham-HIP/The Image Works: p. 4, p. 11 (top), p. 12 (both), p. 20, p. 21, p. 23 (bottom), p. 29 (bottom), p. 30; NMPFT/DHA/SSPL/The Image Works: p. 7 (bottom); SSPL/The Image Works: p.6; Ron Kimball/Ron Kimball Stock: p. 9 (middle left), p. 25 (bottom), p. 26 (top and middle). Other images from stock CD.

Cover: Innovations in race car design from the 1920s were applied to luxury cars, such as this 1930s Duesenberg.

Title page: Starting in 1929, European carmaker Delage introduced its D8 series of sports cars. Like many carmakers, the Great Depression forced this sports and racecar maker to sell to another car company in the 1930s.

Library and Archives Canada Cataloguing in Publication	Library of Congress Cataloging-in-Publication Data

Nielsen, L. Michelle
  Vintage cars / L. Michelle Nielsen.
 	
(Automania!)
Includes index.
ISBN 978-0-7787-3011-8 (bound)
ISBN 0-7787-3011-5 (bound)
ISBN 978-0-7787-3033-0 (pbk.)
ISBN 0-7787-3033-6 (pbk.)
 	
  1. Antique and classic cars--Juvenile literature. 2. Automobiles--History--Juvenile literature. I. Title. II. Series.
 	
TL15.N53 2006   j629.222   C2006-902463-4
	Nielsen, L. Michelle.
	  Vintage cars / written by L. Michelle Nielsen.
	    p. cm. -- (Automania!)
	  Includes bibliographical references and index.
	  ISBN-13: 978-0-7787-3011-8 (rlb : alk. paper)
	  ISBN-10: 0-7787-3011-5 (rlb : alk. paper)
	  ISBN-13: 978-0-7787-3033-0 (pb : alk. paper)
	  ISBN-10: 0-7787-3033-6 (pb : alk. paper)
	  1. Antique and classic cars--Juvenile literature. 2.
	Automobiles--History--Juvenile literature. I. Title. II. Series.
	  TL206.N54 2006
	  629.222--dc22
	
	                                        2006014367

Crabtree Publishing Company

www.crabtreebooks.com   1-800-387-7650

| **Published in Canada**
Crabtree Publishing
616 Welland Ave.
St. Catharines, ON
L2M 5V6 | **Published in the United States**
Crabtree Publishing
PMB16A
350 Fifth Ave., Suite 3308
New York, NY 10118 | **Published in the United Kingdom**
Crabtree Publishing
White Cross Mills
High Town, Lancaster
LA1 4XS | **Published in Australia**
Crabtree Publishing
386 Mt. Alexander Rd.
Ascot Vale (Melbourne)
VIC 3032 |

Contents

The Vintage Years

The vintage car era lasted from the end of World War I, in 1919, until 1930. New advances in car design and engineering were constantly being presented to the public, making this an exciting time in automobile history.

Customer Competition

In the early days of automobiles, carmakers focused on how to make cars work. By 1919, cars were more reliable but there were few options available for buyers. Competition among carmakers became fierce. Each tried to develop ways to make cars better, such as building more powerful engines, safer braking systems, and new, stylish car bodies, so customers would choose their cars. Never had there been so much variety and choice available in cars at every price range. In the United States, almost two million automobiles were produced in 1919. By 1929, that number had more than doubled.

Cheap, Yet Reliable

Many car manufacturers of the era believed that everyone deserved to have a reliable car. To make this happen, more manufacturers mass-produced vehicles, an idea that had first been introduced in car manufacturing by the Ford Motor Company. Mass production was a system of building many cars quickly and cheaply. It allowed reliable cars to be available for affordable prices.

In the 1920s, reliable cars for everyone meant that people's jobs could be farther away from their homes; vacations could be to places that once seemed too far away to travel; and time was saved doing just about anything, including grocery shopping or visiting friends.

Over-the-Top Transportation

In the 1920s, cars were also designed as a way for wealthy customers to show off their power and status. These luxury cars were usually hand-built for the rich and famous. Expensive materials were used, such as gold or silver for car handles and fixtures, walnut wood for interior dashboards and panels, and leather, silk, and other lavish materials for seat coverings. Luxury cars were often equipped with fast and powerful engines for those who loved speed.

(right) The vintage era took place during the "Roaring Twenties," a time when businesses were thriving and many people were wealthy. By the end of the decade, the United States was the richest country in the world thanks to the success of many industries, especially the automobile industry.

The car industry spurred on other industries, which provided jobs and money to many people. Repair shops, gas stations, and drive-through dining are all examples of businesses that did not exist before cars became popular.

Early Automobiles

In the 1800s, automobile inventors based their car designs on horse carriages, with the engine placed beneath the seats. In 1894, a French company, Panhard-Levassor, built a new, more powerful engine underneath a hood and in the front of the car, a design that is still used today.

Assembling Affordable Automobiles

In 1910, only one person out of every 330 owned a car in the United States, and one out of every 600 owned a car in Britain. Cars were still too expensive for average people to buy and maintain. In 1913, American carmaker Henry Ford started an assembly line in his car factory near Dearborn, Michigan. In an assembly line, workers stood in the same spot while parts of the cars passed in front of them on a moving conveyor belt. Each worker was responsible for a specific job, such as attaching a particular part of the car. Before the assembly line, it took twelve and a half hours to build a car at Ford's factory. After the line was introduced, it took only an hour and a half to build one. Assembly lines were cheaper to run than factories that built cars one at a time, which meant that Ford could charge customers less, making his cars more affordable.

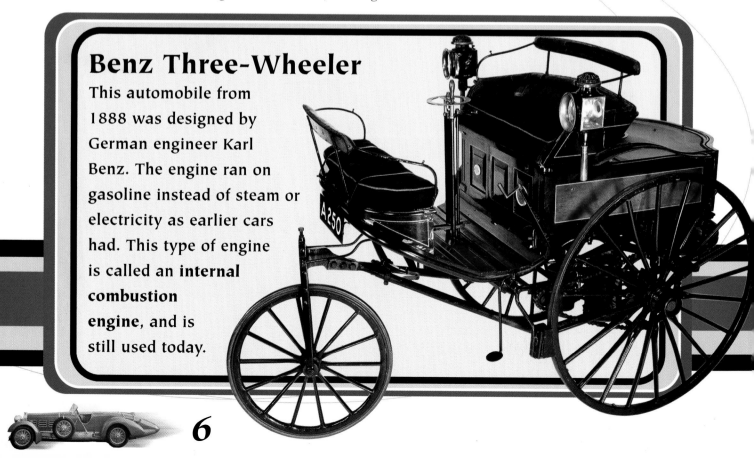

Benz Three-Wheeler

This automobile from 1888 was designed by German engineer Karl Benz. The engine ran on gasoline instead of steam or electricity as earlier cars had. This type of engine is called an **internal combustion engine**, and is still used today.

Automobiles at War

Car manufacturing increased during World War I, a war fought in Europe between 1914 and 1918. Automobiles were needed to transport soldiers and supplies, such as food and weapons, to the **front**. Car manufacturers also made other equipment for the war effort, including airplane engines. Advances in engine design were made to improve the planes used during the war. When the war was over, these engine designs were adapted and applied to car engines.

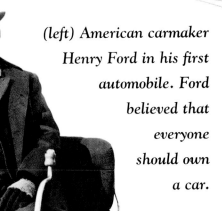

(left) American carmaker Henry Ford in his first automobile. Ford believed that everyone should own a car.

(below) The United States produced 355,000 vehicles in 1912. By 1918, the last year of World War I, production was up to 1,170,000 cars, trucks, and buses. Many of these were used by the military.

Vintage Cars

Many standard features on cars sold at the end of the vintage car era were extras only a decade before. Standard features were parts that automatically came with new cars.

A Typical Tourer

This 1928 Packard tourer shows some of the features and extras of the time. A tourer was an open-styled car with two or four doors and room for four or more passengers. Tourers had either no roof or a cloth roof that folded back. Some had canvas, or cloth, curtains for the windows.

Most cars in the early 1920s were an open style, having a cloth top, and no side windows.

While many cars had hood emblems, or ornaments, luxury cars were known for their beautifully detailed emblems.

Radiator grilles came in different shapes and often had a carmaker's logo on it.

Before the vintage era, most car bodies were made of wood, but carmakers began using steel during the vintage era. Steel was more lightweight, making the car easier to drive.

Many cars had spare tires mounted to the side body panels.

Balloon tires were introduced in the early 1920s. They had wider treads than early tires, which helped in handling and gave a smoother ride.

Body Types

Cars were designed in two pieces. The chassis was the frame the car body was built on, and included the engine, as well as the steering and braking parts. The other part was the car body, which included the hood, fenders, and roof. Many different styles of car bodies could fit on a standard chassis. Here are some common styles of the vintage era:

▶ **Coupe** - A closed body design, or model that has side windows, with two doors, and sometimes comes as a convertible.

◀ **Town Car** - A town car had one closed body compartment for passengers, and one open body compartment for a chauffeur.

▶ **Sedan** - A car style that carried four or more passengers, in a closed body style, and was thought of as a family car.

◀ **Runabout** - A light car that had an open body style, and usually only one bench seat.

▶ **Roadster** - Equipped with two doors, and an open body design, roadsters were often driven down the road with their tops down. Some included a "rumble seat" in the rear, which folded for extra seating.

A Car for Everyone

By 1920, many carmakers had assembly lines in their factories. Car sales grew and buyers had more options to choose from. To stay in business, carmakers had to make sure that their latest model was better than their competitors' cars.

The Popular Model T

The most popular car in the United States during much of the 1920s was also a big seller in Great Britain, France, and Australia. The Ford Model T, or "Tin Lizzie," was made from 1908 to 1927. Over 15 million were sold. Ford's factory assembly line boosted production and cut costs. Starting at $850, the Model T became cheaper until it hit its lowest price of $260 in 1923, a year that recorded sales of two million Model Ts. Although basic in design, the Tin Lizzie was available in nine different body types, including the standard touring car, town car, runabout, and coupe, and in, as Ford joked, "any color you like as long as it's black." At that time, black paint was the only color available that dried quickly enough for assembly line production.

(below) A woman pays for her new car.

Chevrolets on the line at General Motors (GM). In 1923, GM President Alfred Sloan introduced the idea of changing the design of a car model every year. This encouraged people to buy cars more often.

Taking Over the Industry

By the 1920s, large automobile companies, such as General Motors and Ford, dominated the industry. They bought smaller car companies that made different **classes** of cars. By 1920, General Motors had bought Buick, Cadillac, Chevrolet, and Oldsmobile, so they sold cars at every price range. Part of General Motors' plan was to make money on repeat business from their customers. Customers that bought their cheaper cars would hopefully come back when they could afford to buy more expensive models.

(right) The Model T was an easy car to drive. Many American states issued two different drivers licenses: one for Model T drivers and one for everyone else.

11

British Motoring

Across the ocean, Ford ruled the British car industry from 1913 until the mid-1920s, when the Morris Motor Company took reign. Its owner, William Morris, was a British carmaker. Morris' Cowley model came out after World War I, and was nicknamed "the bullnose" because it had a curved front radiator panel. Morris reduced the price of the Cowley in 1921, in part to compete with Ford. Morris established an assembly line in his factory in 1924, which increased the number of cars the company produced and made them more affordable to the British public.

(above) In 1922, the Austin Seven debuted. The car was only 109 inches (277 centimeters) long, but its popularity made the Austin Motorcar Company the second largest car company in Britain.

(right) Like the Ford Model T in the United States, the Austin Seven is credited with making "motoring" popular in Britain, with 250,000 sold in the first year.

(right) The Citroën Model A had a top speed of 40 miles per hour (65 kilometers per hour), but weighed less than a Ford Model T touring car. This meant that the Model A used less fuel.

(below) Carmakers had to advertise to the public to sell their cars. In addition to print ads, Citröen had its name appear in lights on the Eiffel Tower at the opening ceremony of the 1925 Paris International Exhibition.

Citroën Advantage

European car companies adopted the American style of mass production. After visiting the Ford Motor Company, André Citroën, a French inventor, started his own car company in 1919. Citroën was the first European carmaker to set up an assembly line, which produced 100 cars a day in its first year. Citroën's goal was the same as Ford's, to make a car affordable to everyone. Citroën's first car, the four-seater Model A came with standard features, such as an **electric starter**, electric lights, and a spare tire. Most other carmakers charged extra for these parts.

Jobs for Workers

Thousands of jobs were created during the 1920s to keep up with the growing popularity of the car. Carmakers hired more people to build and sell their products, while glass, steel, and rubber companies needed more employees to keep up with orders from carmakers for parts.

On the Line

Building a car requires the skills of designers, who style the bodies, and engineers, who make the engines and other systems work. Many workers are needed to put the pieces together. Before mass production, cars were assembled by highly skilled laborers who knew how to put the entire car together, and even how to make some of the parts. The assembly line allowed workers who did not have a lot of training to get a job at a car factory. In an assembly line, each worker was responsible for one task, such as attaching a part or tightening a bolt. They did the same job all day as the cars moved on conveyer belts in front of them.

Road Workers

The increased number of cars on the roads led to improvements in road conditions. More roads were needed and dirt and gravel roads were paved to prevent cars built low to the ground from getting damaged by potholes, and from getting stuck in the mud. There were also more delivery trucks on the road and their heavy weight damaged road surfaces. Thousands of people were needed in the construction, paving, and design of hard-surfaced roads that could withstand increasing amounts of traffic across North America.

(above) New York City's new line of taxi cars and drivers hired in 1920.

Riding the Car Wave

The car industry had an impact on many other industries, and helped create new businesses. Companies that made products that carmakers needed, such as steel, and car parts, including engines and car bodies, saw business rapidly increase during the 1920s. Gas stations and garages were also built so people could keep their cars running. Hundreds of thousands of people also found jobs in the oil and gas industry. Workers were especially needed in oil fields, where oil was extracted, or taken out of, the ground. People also worked in oil **refineries**, and in building the pipelines that transported the oil across the country.

(below) Ford, General Motors, and Chrysler were "The Big Three" American carmakers of the era. They all had their largest American factories near Detroit, Michigan.

Workers at Ford

Many workers found assembly line work dull and repetitive. The year after Ford introduced the assembly line to his Detroit plant, many of his employees quit. It cost a lot of money to hire employees because each new worker had to be trained. Even new workers did not enjoy working on the assembly line. More than 70 percent of new assembly line workers quit after less than five days on the line. To prevent workers from leaving, Ford more than doubled the hourly wage and reduced shifts from ten hours a day to eight. This helped keep assembly line workers on the job.

Engines and Brakes

Competition among carmakers and the push for new and better technology during World War I helped automobile companies find ways to make cars run better. New advances made cars faster, more powerful, and safer.

Better Brakes

Carmakers looked for ways to improve the safety of their cars. Before the vintage era, most cars had brakes only on their rear wheels. With the increased speeds that cars were capable of, and with the safety of drivers and their families in mind, most carmakers installed four-wheel brakes on their cars by the mid-1920s. To further increase safety, a new type of brake system called **hydraulic brakes** was introduced in 1921. First invented to be used on airplanes, hydraulic brakes applied the braking force evenly on all wheels, which helped prevent skidding.

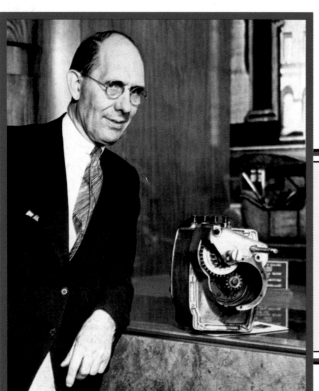

More Powerful Engines

Throughout the 1920s, carmakers introduced cars with more powerful engines. Most low-priced cars in the United States had **four-cylinder engines**. Chevrolet was aware that people who were not wealthy were looking for more power in their cars, so they built a car called the International Six. It was advertised as "A Six for the price of a four," which referred to the number of cylinders its engine had, and let buyers know they were getting more power for less money. Americans bought over one million International Sixes in the first year. Luxury carmakers were also trying to give their customers more cylinders and more power. The Packard Motor Car Company introduced a 12-cylinder engine. In return, their competitor, Cadillac, produced the Cadillac 452, a 16-cylinder automobile, in 1930.

The electric starter was invented in 1911, by Charles Kettering. The starter was widely used in cars during the vintage era. Cars that did not have electric starters had a crank at the front of the car that was turned to start the engine.

Cylinders

Engines are often described by the number of cylinders they have. Car engines are powered by a series of small explosions that take place inside a cylinder. During the vintage era, the easiest way to make a car more powerful, and faster, was to replace the engine with one that had more cylinders. Cylinders can be arranged in a straight line, as in a straight-eight engine, or in a V-formation, which does not take up as much room under the hood.

Super Power

Some luxury car models were equipped with a supercharger, an engine system that gave the car more power, resulting in more speed. Pipes running out of a car's hood meant that the car was supercharged. Superchargers **compressed** air and blew it into the engine, allowing more air to fit into a cylinder. Normally, a mixture of air and gas in the cylinder is ignited, and causes a small explosion to occur, giving power to the car. A supercharger forces air into the engine at a faster rate than normal, which gives each small explosion more power. Superchargers were used in racing cars in the early 1900s, but were first installed in expensive sports cars and luxury cars during the vintage era.

Pontiac belonged to the General Motors company of cars. Its cars first debuted in 1926.

PONTIAC BIG SIX

Advertising Cars

Selling a car in the vintage era was not like selling a car today. Car manufacturers relied heavily on newspaper and magazine advertising, as well as word-of-mouth, to sell their cars. Rather than big, colorful pictures, and short snappy expressions, as is popular in today's ads, the first carmakers felt that they needed to persuade people to invest in their machines. They came up with long, wordy advertisements that explained the values of owning a car built by their company.

Horse or Car?

The automobile was new to people, so car companies had to convince the public that cars would improve their lives and that they were safe to use. When the car was first introduced, its main competition was the horse and buggy. Car companies focused many of their advertisements on the money and time that would be saved if a person decided to give up their horse for an automobile. Oldsmobile, one of the oldest car companies in the United States, claimed that their car would "do the work of six horses at an average cost of $35 a year." Oldsmobile calculated that it cost $180 a year to house and feed a horse. Besides saving $145 a year, an Oldsmobile was also ready to go when their owner was. The same could not be said of a horse.

(above) The hood ornament from a Pierce-Arrow car. Pierce-Arrow made stylish luxury cars.

(right) This 1920s ad was aimed at convincing husbands to buy their wives a car.

Women at the Wheel

At first, car advertising ignored women almost completely. In the traditional family in the early 1900s, women stayed at home to run the household. Car companies saw no point in trying to sell a car to the person who did not work outside the home. By the vintage era, car companies realized not only that women were doing a lot of driving, but also the influence that women had over their families' purchases. Car companies began including women in their promotions, although they still aimed these promotions at men.

Early automobile advertisements contained a lot of text, unlike most of today's advertisements.

A 1929 advertisement for French carmaker Bugatti. In the late 1920s, advertisements became more artistic.

Latest and Greatest

As the public became more willing to accept the car as a reliable form of transportation, car advertisements changed. Owning a luxury car, especially the newest models, was a way to show off a person's status, so many carmakers tried to convince the wealthy that they needed the latest and greatest models. Carmakers advertised the successes that their cars had on the racetrack. Race car drivers were well known by car lovers, and a personal endorsement by a driver helped increase sales.

Car Races

Car racing had been around since 1894, and was originally meant to get people interested in buying cars. In the vintage era, the main reason for car races was still to promote cars, but now carmakers were competing against each other, trying to prove that their cars were number one.

Grand Prix

Grand Prix races were the most popular type of racing and speed testing. The first Grand Prix race took place in France in 1906. By the 1920s, many countries, including Italy, Belgium, and Germany, hosted races. Tracks were built to prevent people from racing their cars on public roads. Cars in Grand Prix races had restrictions placed on them, such as how big their engines could be and how much the cars could weigh. This meant that cars were usually built specifically for racing.

(left) A racecar made by British carmaker W.O. Bentley rounds a corner at the Brooklands track in Surrey, England, in 1929. The driver of the car is Clive Dunfee. Dunfee was part of a group of famous racecar drivers called "the Bentley Boys." The drivers were adored by young people who wanted to become drivers when they were older and by people who simply loved car racing and Bentley cars.

Testing the Engine

A rally was one way to test the **endurance** of cars in the vintage era. These contests tested how well a car worked over long distances. The cars were driven a certain distance in a given time and at a required speed. Drivers lost points if their cars failed at any of these tasks. At the end of the rally, the points were tallied. The winner was the driver with the fewest **penalties**. Rallies were often open to all types of cars, and were held on public roads. Other endurance races were held that required a car to travel long distances without stopping, although the distances were not as long as in rallies.

(above) Until 1970, each Le Mans race started with the drivers running to their cars in a foot race. They then started their engines and were off.

24 Hours at Le Mans

The most famous endurance race was the Le Mans 24 Hour Race. The first Le Mans 24 Hour Race was held in 1923 in Le Mans, France. Racing cars were becoming so specialized in the 1920s that race organizers noticed that fewer spectators were coming to watch speed races that used cars they could never hope to drive. Le Mans was only open to cars that anyone could buy. Drivers had to keep their cars running for 24 hours with the winner having the highest average speed and traveling the greatest distance. Most cars that drove in Le Mans had an open design, and were four-seater touring cars. Any work that needed to be done on the car during the race, such as changing tires, was done by the driver.

Sports Cars

Sports cars became popular in the 1920s. Sports cars have smaller, lighter bodies, and can be driven faster than other types of cars.

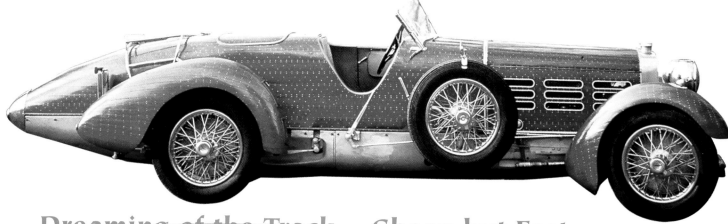

Dreaming of the Track

Automotive companies used the public's love for racing to sell cars. Sports car owners were usually car racing fans who wanted racecar features in their everyday cars. Italian carmakers, such as Fiat, Alfa Romeo, and Bugatti developed a reputation for building winning racecars, but they made a lot of money by selling sports cars to the public. When a car manufacturer had a winning racecar, it improved the image of all the cars that manufacturer made, which led to an increase in sales.

Cheap but Fast

Very expensive sports cars were handcrafted, and bought by rich people who wanted to show off their wealth. By the late 1920s, some carmakers began building lower priced sports cars for those people who wanted a car with the qualities that sports cars had become known for, such as the capability for high speeds, and a low, sleek body design.

(above) This 1924 sports car was handcrafted by European carmaker Hispano-Suiza.

(right) The Bugatti Type 35 was a successful racing car. Bugatti came out with a less expensive sports car version, the Type 37, that had the same look of the Type 35, but was cheaper.

The MG Car Company used car parts that had been used in regular mass-produced cars and built light, two-seater bodies on their low-priced sports cars. The MG Midget was a cheap sports car introduced in 1928. It was an instant hit.

American Speed

In the United States, sports cars were developed from early **speedsters**, which were lightweight cars capable of high speeds. To create a racecar, many carmakers took the chassis, or frame, and engine they used for their mass-produced vehicles and combined it with a two-seater body that was lighter and could go faster than a heavy body with the same amount of power. A popular American speedster was the Auburn 8-90 made by the Auburn Automobile Company. Introduced in 1928, the Auburn 8-90 was known for its high speeds and long curved fenders. The car, while priced lower than competing models, was one of Auburn's more expensive cars at $1,895. Its reputation as a racecar that held world records helped make it a successful model for Auburn.

(below) In 1927, race car driver Henry Segrave (left) became the first person to drive a car at over 200 miles per hour (322 kilometers per hour).

Luxury Cars

Expensive luxury cars were often as famous as the people who drove them. Buying a flashy, luxurious vehicle was a way to show off wealth. Customers wanted all the new technologies, such as the most powerful engines on the market, and the latest handcrafted car body designs.

Wanting It All

Large car companies were often separated into divisions, with each division building a different class of car. Henry Ford's son, Edsel, wanted the Ford Motor Company to sell cars in the luxury class. In 1922, he convinced his father to buy the failing Lincoln Motor Company, which already had a reputation for building well-made luxury vehicles. Edsel Ford brought in some of the best **coachbuilders** to redesign the Lincoln's look. Lincolns were a popular choice in American luxury cars and were driven by many famous people, including U.S. President Herbert Hoover.

Packing It In

Some car companies specialized in making only luxury cars, such as the Packard Motor Car Company. The Packard Twin Six, a car with an advanced 12-cylinder engine, was introduced before the vintage era but remained popular into the early 1920s. It gave Packard a reputation for luxury cars that rivaled Lincoln. When the **Great Depression** hit in 1929, fewer people had the money to buy luxury cars. Lincoln survived on the support from the bigger company that owned it. Packard started to build more affordable cars, but their reputation as a luxury carmaker never fully recovered after the Depression ended.

An advertisement for Lincoln, which was owned by the Ford Motor Company.

Building a Luxury Car

Pierce-Arrow was a name that people all over the world associated with luxury vehicles. The American company, which entered car manufacturing in 1901, had a reputation for producing cars that were well-tested for reliability and performance. Before a Pierce-Arrow vehicle left the assembly plant, each engine was disassembled for inspection and every car was driven to ensure that it was in perfect condition. The Series 33 was the flagship, or most well-known, vehicle for Pierce-Arrow in the early 1920s.

(below) The Pierce-Arrow was the first car to have its headlights mounted directly into the car's front fenders. This feature was introduced in 1913 and became a characteristic that people used to identify a Pierce-Arrow car.

Pierce-Arrows were driven by a number of American celebrities, including movie star Ginger Rogers (above), baseball legend Babe Ruth, and inventor Orville Wright, who is credited with building the first airplane.

Introduced in 1928, the American-made Duesenberg Model J was built with only the best parts. Designed to be above and beyond anything else on the road, the Model J's price was higher than any other car.

The Perfect Car?

One of the most renowned luxury carmakers was the British company, Rolls-Royce. All Rolls-Royce cars lived up to the glamorous look of luxury cars but how they worked was most important to Henry Royce, the engineer responsible for Rolls-Royce cars. Royce believed a car should run smoothly, quietly, and forever, and any mechanical problem was quickly fixed at no charge. Rolls-Royce customers included European royalty, political leaders, Indian **maharajahs**, and other extremely wealthy individuals. In 1925, the expensive Phantom I was introduced. It sold over 2,200 models in its four years of production.

(above) A 1925 Rolls-Royce Piccadilly Roadster.

Italian Luxury

Engineers at Isotta-Fraschini used their wartime experience to create powerful engines for their luxury automobiles. Introduced in 1919, the Tipo 8 was Isotta-Fraschini's first large-sized luxury car. Often driven by a chauffeur, the Tipo 8 became a favorite among royalty. The Tipo 8 was built until 1924, when it was replaced by the Tipo 8A, a vehicle with an even larger, more powerful engine.

(below) Italian-made Isotta-Fraschinis were popular luxury cars in the United States.

Glam Cars

To drive a Hispano-Suiza in the 1920s was to drive the most glamorous car available. Hispano-Suiza was a European carmaker that used its experience building warplane engines in World War I to improve the power of its automobiles. Powerful engines, along with the latest in four-wheel brake systems, made Hispano-Suiza cars more advanced than other luxury cars, including Rolls-Royce. The H6 was introduced to the world in 1919 as one of the most advanced cars available with the latest four-wheel brakes and a top-of-the-line six-cylinder engine. The open body design was considered by many to be a work of art, but the H6 was only available to the very wealthy.

Car of Kings

The Bugatti Royale, or Type 40, was a car designed for royalty. At over 14 feet (four meters) long, its unusual design, which included a front hood longer than some small cars, and power to reach 200 miles per hour (320 kilometers per hour), demanded attention from any onlooker. Ettore Bugatti had always wanted to build a car that surpassed the reputation of the Rolls-Royce to become the most talked-about vehicle in the world. The great success of the Bugatti racing team in 1926 gave Ettore the money he needed to build his dream car. He succeeded in making a classic automobile that would always be remembered, but not a car that would make it into many driveways. The Royale was three times more expensive than its Rolls-Royce competitor, which explains why only three out of the six cars made were sold. Bugatti offered customers a lifetime guarantee on the Royale.

The Bugatti family ended up keeping unsold Royales for their own use. The Royale has lived up to its claim of lasting forever, as all six that were made are still around today.

Vintage Cars Today

The important cars of the vintage era are still appreciated by many people. Vintage cars were built with materials that lasted longer than previous materials, including metal rather than wood car bodies. Many vintage cars are still on the road today. Car collectors often make a hobby out of restoring, or fixing up, these cars.

A Passion for Vintage

Vintage car lovers, like anyone with a hobby, enjoy talking about their passion with others that feel the same way. All over the world, people form clubs or groups for the purpose of appreciating vintage cars. These groups are based in a certain area, with members getting together regularly for events and meetings. Some groups have members from across the country or even the world, who share information about vintage cars through the Internet or vintage car newsletters.

(below) Car shows and events that display vintage cars educate people on this important era in automotive history.

(above) Restoring a vintage car requires a lot of time and research. Car systems worked differently than those in modern cars, and many of the materials used in car bodies and parts are not the same as today's.

A Sporting Chance

The Vintage Sports Car Club of Great Britain formed in 1934, just 4 years after the vintage era had ended. The club's founders felt that mass production meant the end of proper car building, and they wanted to preserve and continue to compete in vintage sports cars. Today, there are over 7,500 members from all over the world. Many members come to the events organized by the Vintage Sports Car Club to watch or compete in different car events, including racing, hill climb trials, driving tests, and sprints.

Some vintage car owners drive their vehicles around their towns or neighborhoods, treating them as a form of transportation, while others rarely drive their cars, having them because they are an important piece of the past. Here, a vintage car takes part in a hill climb, a type of race in which drivers race to the top of a hill.

Car designers and engineers who worked during the vintage era had the vision that allowed cars to change lives. Whether bringing an affordable car to the market, or building the fastest car in the world, carmakers during the 1920s ensured that their cars would hold a permanent place in history.

Building an Empire

Errett Lobban Cord bought the Auburn Automobile Company and saved the struggling manufacturer by selling over 2,000 cars that were sitting unsold from the previous year. Auburn built a new lineup of cars to appeal to buyers looking for quality. Expanding his automotive empire, Cord also purchased the Duesenberg Motor Company in 1926, and just two years later, the famous Model J debuted. After a few unsuccessful cars, Cord shut down his empire in 1937.

Britain's Carmaker

William Morris owned a bicycle shop, followed by a motorcycle, and then a car business. At his garage in Oxford, England, he repaired and sold vehicles made by other carmakers. Convinced he could make a better car, Morris came out with the Morris Oxford in 1912. Morris did not build the entire car himself, but instead bought parts from other British companies. The Oxford met Morris' goal of building a good quality car that was also cheap. Building affordable cars became an important idea of Morris Motors.

Ettore Bugatti is known by car lovers as one of the best designers of luxury and racing cars.

W.O. Bentley

Walter Owen Bentley (below) was an engineer. His first job with cars was with the National Cab Company, in London, where he helped make sure all the taxis were in good condition. Bentley designed the first engine that had aluminum **pistons**, which was used during World War I to power airplanes. After the war, Bentley wanted to design and build his own cars, so he formed Bentley Motors in 1919. His company became known as one of the best manufacturers of race and luxury cars. The Bentley company was taken over by Rolls-Royce in 1931.

(below) William Morris brought the American-born idea of mass production to Britain, opening up the roads for countless British drivers.

Fewer Cars

Fred and August Duesenberg immigrated to the United States from Germany. For many years, the brothers worked fixing and building engines. The Duesenberg Automobile and Motor Company was started in 1919, and it quickly became a leading car manufacturer. Duesenberg cars had the latest in mechanical features, including engines and brake systems. The brothers were not interested in mass production methods and so each Duesenberg was built by hand, specially for each client. Over the company's 19-year life, fewer than 650 sporting and touring cars were made.

Glossary

class Car grouping based on size or body style

coachbuilders People who specialized in building the body of a car

compressed Packed tightly together

electric starter A device that starts the engine

endurance The amount of time and distance that an automobile can run for

engineering Applying science to design and build structures and machines

four-cylinder engine An internal combustion engine with four cylinders

front The area where the main fighting in a war is taking place

Grand Prix races Road races for automobiles that originally tested vehicle endurance

Great Depression A period of global economic hardship during the 1930s

hydraulic brake A braking system that uses pressure applied to a fluid, usually a type of oil, to slow down a vehicle

internal combustion engine A type of engine that uses a spark to ignite a fuel, creating an explosion that forces other engine parts to move

maharajah An Indian prince

penalty A mark against a competitor

piston A plug that moves up and down in a cylinder

radiator Part of the cooling system of a vehicle

refinery A place where substances are separated into different parts

speedster A type of car with two seats and usually no roof, also called a roadster

World War I An international conflict that lasted from 1914 until 1918 and was fought mostly in Europe

Index

Printed in the U.S.A.